THE
SEA OF GALILEE

PALPHOT LTD.

INTRODUCTION

Since early times, the Land of Israel has been held sacred by numerous nations and religions. For those who yearned to visit, this land was the center of the universe. Since the late 1st century C.E. the northern strip of the country has been an important center, and was therefore known as the Land of Galilee (from the Hebrew root "to roll" - thus suggesting a circle).

The uniqueness of the Galilee is found in its unusual topography, its climate, its flora and fauna, its important international trade routes, enchanting landscapes, and in the intoxicating atmosphere of its historical sites. The famous American writer Mark Twain described the Galilee in "The Innocents Abroad" as follows:

"In the starlight, Galilee has no boundaries but the broad compass of the heavens, and is a theater meet for great events; meet for the birth of a religion able to save a world: and meet for the stately Figure appointed to stand upon its stage and proclaim its high decrees...."

From the time Jesus and His disciples arrived in the Galilee, the region also became sacred to Christianity. This was the period during which many of the most well known of the miracles of Jesus were performed. *"And after these things, Jesus went away to the other side of the Sea of Galilee which is the sea of Tiberias. And a great multitude followed him, because they beheld signs which he did on them that were sick"* (John 10.1-2).

Following the destruction of Jerusalem in the year 70 B.C., the Patriarchate and the Sanhedrin were reestablished in Tiberias, thereby transferring the spiritual-national center of the Jewish nation to the Galilee.

The beauty of the Sea of Galilee (Kinneret) region - which combines enchanting scenery with religious splendor and sanctity - is recognized throughout the world.

The Jordan River which feeds the Sea of Galilee is also considered holy by the Christians. In the year 1170 a well-known traveler to the Land of Israel wrote:

"It is the custom of the Christians at the close of the Passover festival to participate in a mass pilgrimage from Jerusalem to the Jordan River. When they reach the River, they immerse themselves in the holy waters. Many wear white clothing during the baptismal ceremony, after which they put on festive clothing, fill their bottles with the pure water and return to Jerusalem".

There are few places in the world where such breathtaking landscapes so inspired writers and poets. Among all the sites serving as such a source of inspiration, the Sea of Galilee emerges as queen.

The first Christian pilgrims to make their way to the holy sites in the Land of Israel set out as early as the 2nd century C.E. They were most interested in the sacred sites; the beautiful scenery was secondary in importance.

Salah Maril's 19th century travelogue describing his travels to the Holy Land represents the renewal of the pilgrimage movement to the Land of Israel and to the Sea of Galilee region. He wrote in 1877:

"One of the most beautiful sights in the world is the Sea of Galilee, as seen from the height of the mountains.... It is as if the Sea of Galilee were at our feet... the surface of the water is radiant under the blue skies, completely calm and spectacularly lovely. As the sea is surrounded by hills, it appears more like a work of art than a natural body of water."

Since the 19th century, the region has become an international tourist center, and the focus of pilgrimages to Christian and Jewish holy sites. The modern city of Tiberias thrives on tourism, many hotels of all categories provide accommodation for pilgrims and holidaymakers.

Let us now follow in the footsteps of our ancestors and visit some of the ancient sites near the Sea of Galilee.

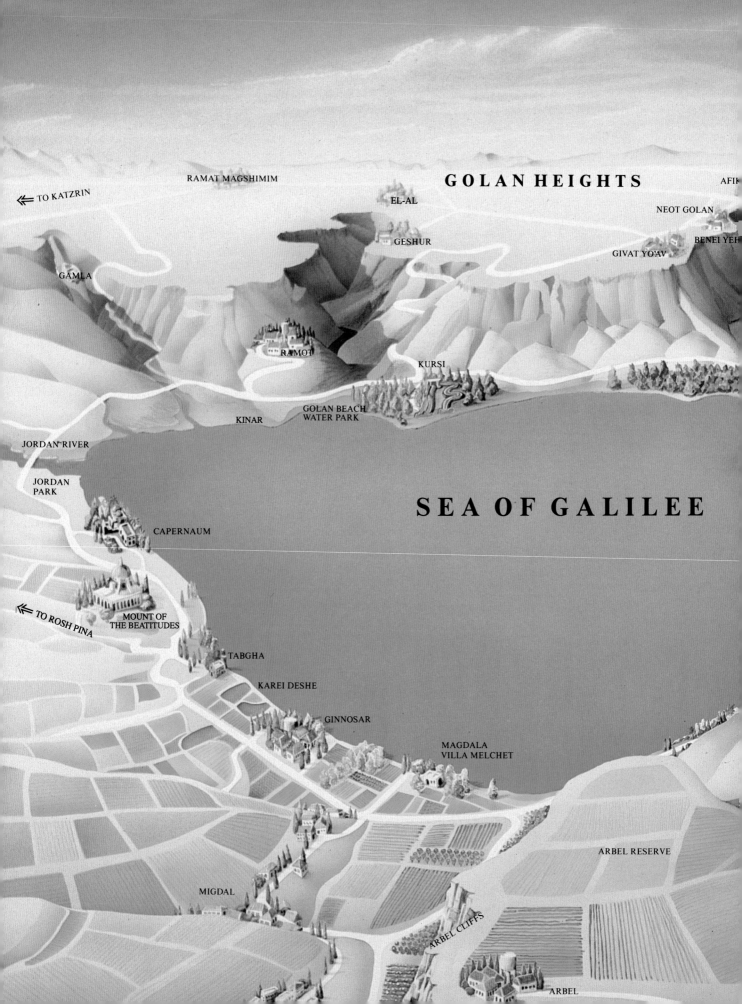

RAMAT MAGSHIMIM

GOLAN HEIGHTS

AFIK

← TO KATZRIN

EL-AL

NEOT GOLAN

GESHUR

BENEI YEH

GIVAT YO'AV

GAMLA

RAMOT

KURSI

KINAR

GOLAN BEACH
WATER PARK

JORDAN RIVER

JORDAN
PARK

SEA OF GALILEE

CAPERNAUM

← TO ROSH PINA

MOUNT OF
THE BEATITUDES

TABGHA

KAREI DESHE

GINNOSAR

MAGDALA
VILLA MELCHET

ARBEL RESERVE

MIGDAL

ARBEL CLIFFS

ARBEL

YARMUK RIVER

HAMMAT GADER

KFAR HARUV

MEVO HAMMA

SITA

TEL KATZIR

EIN GEV

HA'ON

MA'AGAN

ZEMACH

DEGANIA

KINNERET

TIBERIAS HOT SPRINGS

YARDENIT

TIBERIAS

UPPER TIBERIAS

KFAR HITTIM

TO AFULA

City of Tiberias on the Sea of Galilee

April 22nd 1839

TIBERIAS

Tiberias is located on the western shore of the Sea of Galilee. The city was founded between the years 18 C.E. and 20 C.E. by King Herod Antipas and named in honor of his friend the Roman Emperor Tiberius. In the 5th-6th centuries Tiberias was at its peak, as the capital of the Galilee and the spiritual center of the Jewish nation. Today Tiberias is an international tourist center, in close proximity to all the holy sites in the Galilee.

The city is built up from the Sea of Galilee - which lies at 212 meters below sea level, to a height of 220 meters above sea level. To the east are the hills of the Golan, to the north the hills of Galilee and the city of Safed, and to the south the Jordan Valley.

Since its founding, Tiberias was a walled city. After an earthquake destroyed the city in 1033, a Crusader general reestablished the city north of the original site (see Roberts' 19th century illustration). The towers were built right into the Sea of Galilee to prevent the waters of the sea from washing up over the shoreline. Tiberias was a city at an important crossroads on the routes between Egypt and Damascus (Syria), Egypt and Beirut (Lebanon), and between Jerusalem and Safed.

Today, the tower houses restaurants, shops and an interesting tourist spot known as "The Galilee Experience" - an audiovisual presentation of the story of the Galilee and the Sea of Galilee and their historical and religious significance.

Opposite this tower is a structure which served as a mosque for over 150 years. Since 1948 and to this

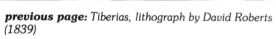

previous page: Tiberias, lithograph by David Roberts (1839)
opposite: Tiberias from the south
above: The promenade
below right: Partial view of modern Tiberias
below left: The Tiberias museum

Jordan River   Moriah Plaza   Caesar

day, it houses a museum which recounts the history of Tiberias and the Sea of Galilee. In 1992 the museum's directorate decided to preserve the mosque in its original form.

As we continue along the promenade, we can almost reach out and touch the water. Tourist boats and a few fishing boats are docked in the marina. Restaurant tables adorn the entire length of the promenade, inviting visitors to taste the excellent fish of the Sea of Galilee.

At any hour of the day you can sail out into the sea. Looking from east to west beyond the city, you can observe how the city is nestled in the hilly landscape

Lido

Galilee Experience

along the seashore. At night the view of the snake of lights winding its way between the mountains until it reaches the sea is particularly breathtaking. One can easily distinguish between the larger hotels prominently marking the seashore and the smaller buildings, and enjoy the lights reflected on the water in a blaze of color.

above: The promenade with some of the hotels
above right: the " Galilee Experience" offers a panorama of Tiberias history
right: Water Skiing
below left: Ancient mosaic from the 6th century Synagogue in the archeological park.

Following the great flood of 1934, the British built a promenade along the entire shore of the city. Walking along this esplanade the stroller can observe the restaurants, the boat docks, and several ancient houses. Among these houses is an Arab mosque called the Mosque of the Sea (Jam'a Al Ba'hir) which today houses a museum chronicling the history of the city.

Beyond the promenade and its row of restaurants are Tiberias' modern hotels - Galei Kinneret, Plaza, River Jordan, Caesar - and among them an archaeological park. The municipal tourist bureau is housed in a reconstructed ancient building in the center of this park. In the park itself one can examine the remnants of an ancient 6th century synagogue which was destroyed in the earthquake of 749; at the center of the prayer hall is an exquisite mosaic floor decorated with sacred fruits and the name of the donor - Prikulus ben Krispus.

Walking back to the promenade, one comes across the only surviving synagogue in the Jewish Quarter (the Jews' Courtyard). Submerged in the water at the southern end of the promenade is a tower from the city's ancient wall. Situated on a site once sacred to the Jews, a Greek Orthodox Church today occupies the tower.

CITY OF SAGES AND BURIAL SITE OF SAINTS

As we walk uphill we come across the grave of Rabbi Meir Ba'al Ha'ness (the Miracle Worker) who lived in Tiberias in the 2nd century A.D. Jews from all parts of Israel and pilgrims from across the world travel to his graveside to recite special prayers of supplication for peace and good health. In the past, a procession would leave Tiberias, led by men carrying the scrolls of the Torah; upon arriving at the grave of Meir Ba'al Ha'ness they would rejoice in a great festivity.

Tiberias is the burial site of other famous Jewish sages, among them Rabbi Akiva, Rabbi Yohanan ben Zakkai, and Maimonides (the Ramban) - the famous philosopher and physician. Throughout the year pilgrims visit Maimonides' grave, which is located within the city.

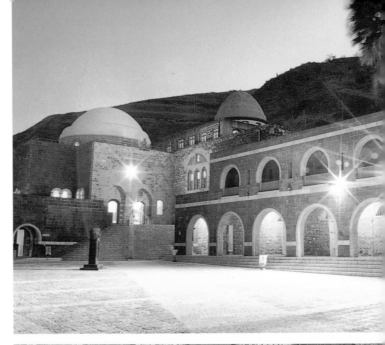

HAMMEI TIBERIAS

Herod Antipas had good reason to establish a city in Tiberias, as the neighboring town, Hammat, was blessed with hot springs. Soldiers of the Roman legions, and centuries later, the Crusaders, came to Hammat to enjoy these hot springs, which are still operative today. The area has earned international repute as a healing center with modern facilities and services.

Ancient and modern bathhouses near the hot springs are also in use. Alongside the ancient bathhouses is a small museum which contains a reconstruction of an ancient bathing room.

HAMMAT EXCAVATIONS

Two ancient synagogues, containing important archaeological finds, were uncovered in Hammat; among the finds was a 7-branched menorah (candelabrum) carved from stone. The floor of one of the synagogues is decorated with an exquisite mosaic; at its center is the wheel of the zodiac (the earliest known artistic depiction uncovered in Israel,) and the Greek sun-god Helios.

opposite above: Tiberias, the modern hot springs
left: Ancient Roman hot springs
above right: Grave of Rabbi Meir Ba'al Ha'ness
right: Detail from zodiac mosaic at the ancient Synagogue, Hammat
below right: The zodiac mosaic at the ancient Synagogue, Hammat
overleaf - page 14
above left: Tiberias, the ancient citadel
above right: The church on the hill of Biriniki
below: the archeological park
overleaf - page 15: Views of Tiberias at night
overleaf - page 16: Tiberias, general view from the south

We are leaving Tiberias, the capital of the Galilee, to visit other important sites in the vicinity of the Sea of Galilee. Wherever we turn - south or north, wherever our feet touch the ground, we come across interesting sites which integrate the past and the present.

Traveling northward, at the very northern edge of the city we come across the Scottish church, built in the late 19th century by Dr.Torrance. It is worthwhile to visit the unique buildings and oriental gardens which cover the church grounds. Two minutes from the Scottish church, we come across the Russian church and the YMCA, hidden in lush green gardens on the lower slopes of Tiberias.

VALLEY OF GINOSSAR

As we drive along the northern shores toward the Valley of Ginossar, we pass the spot Napoleon visited in 1799 during his failed attempt to wrest the Holy Land from the Turks. As the Valley of Ginossar was a well-known region in ancient times, the Sea of Galilee was often referred to as the Sea of Ginossar.

MAGDALA

Magdala was the birthplace of Mary Magdalene, and the place where she met with Jesus. In those times, Magdala was the most important city in the Sea of Galilee region (before Tiberias was founded), and the home of 45,000 residents. The city was famed for its fish industry; excavations in the area have uncovered beautiful mosaics with illustrations of the fish trade and of fishing boats. It is easy to understand why Jesus and His disciples settled in this area.

JESUS' BOAT

At a walking distance from Magdala, right on the seashore, is Kibbutz Ginossar, located on the site of a very ancient settlement.

In 1985, after 10 years of drought, large areas of the Sea of Galilee had dried up. An ancient wooden boat was discovered in the sand, it has been conclusively identified by researchers the world over as a boat dating to the time of Jesus. The boat is on display in Beit Allon, next to Kibbutz Ginossar.

previous page 17 - above: Tiberias with Mt. Hermon in the background
below: Mt. Arbel with the Sea of Galilee
opposite page 18 - left: Aerial view of Kibbutz Ginossar with the hotel and Allon House
right: Mt. Arbel

As we stand in the Valley of Ginossar we look up and observe the Cliff of Arbel and Karnei Hittin. We now continue northward. The famous river, Wadi Amud, ends not far from here, and if we climb towards it we can face south and view the Valley of Ginossar from the north.

At this point we leave the western banks of the Sea of Galilee and travel northward. We leave the Valley of Ginossar and the landscapes of Magdala and turn our view towards the northern banks of the Sea, a region replete with Christian holy sites.

above left: Remains of 4th century Synagogue on Mt. Arbel
above right: The Galilee boat - now preserved and housed in a museum
below left: Wadi Amud
below right: Mosaic from Magdala - depicting ancient boat

FIRST CENT. A.D. From MAGDALA

above: *The exterior of the Church of the Multiplication of the Loaves and the Fishes, Tabgha*

below: *The interior of the Church of the Multiplication of the Loaves and the Fishes, Tabgha*

TABGHA

The first place we stop is Tabgha, where we come across remnants of ancient sites sacred to Jews and Christians. The name Tabgha is a distortion of the Greek word Heptapegon which means "Seven Springs"; this also explains the Hebrew name Ein Sheva ("Spring of Seven"). In the past, seven springs met at this point, and flowed into the Sea of Galilee; today only five remain.

The "Seven Springs" became known to the Christian world as the result of two miracles which, according to Christian tradition, took place here. The first was the miracle of the five loaves of bread and the two fish, with which Jesus was able to feed 5,000 people. (Matthew 14:16-21).

The second miracle was the revelation of Jesus to His disciples, the fishermen, after His death, and the announcement of Peter's primacy over the other disciples in Jesus' commandment to Peter to "feed my sheep." (John 21:16).

Shortly after Christianity was declared the official religion of the Byzantine Empire in the year 320 C.E., messengers were sent to all corners of the empire to establish churches. The Holy Land was marked as the major objective, and the home of Jesus and his disciples near the Sea of Galilee - the jewel in the crown. The first church was built here in 350, and upon its ruins the Church of the Multiplication of the Loaves and the Fishes stands today.

The church contains an early mosaic floor with illustrations of the basket of loaves and the two fish. It also depicts birds, peacocks, (the symbol of eternity), the lotus flower and other plants. This is considered to be one of the most beautiful mosaics in all of Israel.

above right: *Dalmanutha prayer site, on the west side of the sea of Galilee*

below and opposite: *Details from the mosaic floor of Tabgha*

MOSAIC IN THE CHURCH OF THE MULTIPLICATION OF THE LOAVES AND THE FISHES

Many mosaic floors have been uncovered in the Land of Israel, but few are as beautiful and colorful in their illustrations of the fauna and flora of lakes and swamps. In the mosaic, one can easily identify ducks, herons and cormorants.

The two churches - the ancient and the new - are located adjacent to the springs and a flour mill from the Byzantine period. The historical and religious associations of the place, make it emotionally moving to Christian visitors.

above: Decorations on the entrance door to the Church of the Multiplication of the Loaves and the Fishes
below right: *View from Tabgha towards the Sea of Galilee and Mt. Arbel*

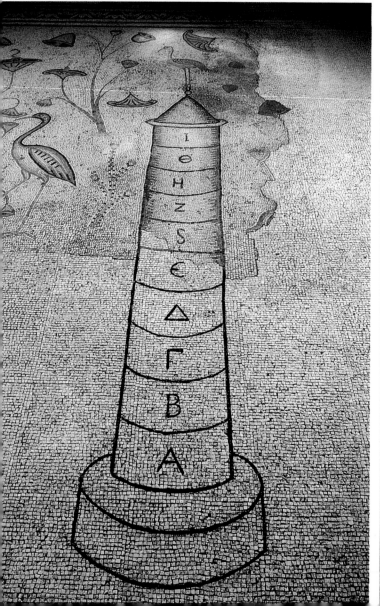

above: Bird's eye view of the Church of St. Peter's
Primacy with the Mt. of Beatitudes in the background

ST. PETER'S CHURCH

Near the Church of the Multiplication, next to ancient
steps leading down to the waterline stands St. Peter's
Church, also called the Chapel of St. Peter's Primacy.
It was built by the Franciscans in 1938, on Byzantine
foundations, and is still cared for by them today. The
stark simplicity of the Church is enhanced by the black
basalt rocks used in its construction. The Church
encloses the rock known as Mensa Christi - the Table
of Christ. Here Jesus "showed himself again to his
disciples at the sea of Tiberias". (John 21:1), and they
ate together.

opposite above: Pilgrims outside the Church of St. Peter's Primacy, Tabgha

below: Interior of the Church of St. Peter's Primacy, Tabgha

above: Fishermen in front of the Church of St. Peter's Primacy

below left: Statue overlooking the Sea of Galilee. This statue depicts Christ, after the Resurrection, appearing for the third time before His disciples.

overleaf
The Sea of Galilee

CAPERNAUM

Imagine yourself on a trip to the Holy Land, looking for a pastoral spot in a fishing village on a lake, with the sacred atmosphere of days gone by! No place fits the description better than the Valley of Saida in Capernaum. This famous ancient fishing village was the home of Peter the fisherman (one of the twelve apostles), where Jesus lived while He was based in the Galilee. In the ancient synagogue in Capernaum Jesus preached, in its alleys He cured the sick, and at the fishermen's wharf He performed his wondrous miracles. Excavations in the area have uncovered the remnants of the famous Jewish village from the Roman period. The reconstructed synagogue and the ancient church which stand side by side recall the Byzantine period when Jews and early Christians lived together harmoniously in the same village.

The ancient synagogue, built in the 3rd century and restored in the 5th century, was built of beautifully hewn white limestone. The white color is particularly impressive against the black basalt stone from

which the surrounding homes were constructed. The walls of the structure are finely carved with geometric ornamentations and decorations depicting plants and animals. A Holy Ark, decorated with Jewish ceremonial symbols, was found in the synagogue.

previous - page 31:
Part of the ancient Synagogue at Capernaum

opposite - page 32:
Bird's eye view of Capernaum and the Sea of Galilee, showing the family living quarters and the new church covering Peter's house.

above - right and below:
Remains of the ancient Synagogue on which Jewish symbols are carved . The menorah and the relief of a jug with bunches of grapes can clearly be seen.

overleaf - page 34:
Columns of the ancient Synagogue - which is probably built on the site of the original building where Jesus preached during His Galilean Ministry.

overleaf - page 35 - above:
External view of new church at Capernaum

below:
Interior of the new church at Capernaum
The modern church is usually kept closed. It is only opened by special request for groups of Catholic pilgrims who wish to celebrate Mass.

opposite - page 36:

above: Carvings on the Synagogue in Capernaum showing Jewish symbols, such as palm branches and pomegranates.

below: Partial view of the ancient Synagogue

above right:

A relief from the Synagogue showing the carriage for carrying the Holy Ark of the Covenant.

above left:

Stone pillar with roughly engraved inscription.

below:

To the left of the picture is a mill for breaking olives, and to the right an oil press - which can also be used to make flour.

MOUNT OF BEATITUDES

Overlooking the northern shore of the Sea of Galilee is the Mount of Beatitudes where, according to Christian tradition, Jesus delivered the Sermon on the Mount and chose His apostles from among His disciples. From the balcony of the monastery and the Italian church which were built on this site, one has an enchanting view of the northern part of the Sea, the cliffs of the Golan Heights and the mountains of the Lower Galilee. Peace and tranquility encompass the spot.

The place was named Mount of Beatitudes after the word Ashrei ("blessed") with which Jesus began each of the eight sections of His Sermon on the Mount:

Blessed are the poor in spirit: for theirs is the kingdom of heaven.
Blessed are they that mourn: for they shall be comforted.
Blessed are the meek: for they shall inherit the earth.
Blessed are they that hunger and thirst after righteousness: for they shall be filled.
Blessed are the merciful: for they shall obtain mercy.
Blessed are the pure in heart: for they shall see God.

Blessed are the peacemakers: for they shall be called sons of God.

Blessed are they that have been persecuted for righteousness' sake: for theirs is the kingdom of heaven. (Matthew 5:3-10).

The church structure was completed in 1938 with a contribution made by A.N.S.M.I. Antonio Barluzzi, the architect, designed the building with eight wings, representing the eight verses in the Sermon on the Mount.

previous - page 38:

above: *Partial view of the ancient synagogue*

below right: *The Greek Orthodox Church at Capernaum*

below left: *Statue of "The Canticle of Creatures", St. Francis of Assisi*

page 39

View of the Sea of Galilee and the Church of the Beatitudes

opposite - page 40 - above: *The high altar in the Church of the Beatitudes*

above: *The Cupola of the Church of the Beatitudes - part of the text of each of the eight Beatitudes is written on each window of the Cupola.*

overleaf - pages 42 & 43: *Views of the Church of the Beatitudes*

THE JORDAN PARK

We face southward, and observe a breathtaking view of the Sea of Galilee. The hills of the Golan are to the east, the cliff of Arbel to the west, and at our feet is the Jordan River as it enters the Sea of Galilee, one of the few places along the length of the river which is accessible to visitors - a site for prayer and baptism.

Possibly the most famous river in the world - the Jordan is mentioned many times in the Bible: - "Jesus baptized of John in Jordan," (Mark 1:9). Joshua and the Children of Israel "passed clean over Jordan". (Joshua 3:17). are just two references.

The Jordan Park provides shady picnic areas and secluded spots to relax and enjoy the peaceful surroundings under the welcome shade of the trees. It is a Nature Preservation Reserve - one of many in Israel.

above: The Jordan Park
below: The River Jordan entering the Sea of Galilee in the Betecha valley

KORAZIN

Korazin, like Capernaum, was a prosperous and flourishing Jewish village in the Byzantine period. As befitted a wealthy community, its residents erected a beautiful and elaborate synagogue of black basalt stone, which has been restored in recent times. Part of the stone frieze and the surrounding architectural remains are decorated with geometric designs, and with patterns incorporating local flowers and animals.

According to Christian tradition, Jesus cursed this city, along with Beit Saida and Capernaum, as the inhabitants refused to accept His teachings.

Returning to the path which winds along the northern shore of the Sea of Galilee, we pass the mouth of the Jordan River, the point where it enters the Sea. We approach the slopes of the Golan Heights towards the eastern shore of the Sea, where we arrive at another important Christian site.

above: *Remains of the ancient Synagogue of Korazin*
below: *Remains of ancient houses*

KURSI

A monastery and a church were established on this site in the mid 5th century. The prayer hall in the church was built in the form of a basilica. A room on one side of the nave was used for Baptism ceremonies. At the entrance to this room a Greek inscription from 585 C.E. was found, indicating that it was built at the time of Stephanus, the head of the Monastery, and King Mauricanus.

According to tradition, this was the place where the "Miracle of the Swine" was performed. Jesus cured a sick man by driving the evil spirits which possessed him into a herd of local swine. The crazed animals ran towards the nearby Sea of Galilee and drowned.

opposite above: *Two views of the ancient Church at Kursi*
below: *Tel Hadar and the Sea of Galilee*
above and below: *Touring boats on the Sea of Galilee*

KIBBUTZ EIN GEV

As afternoon approaches, we hurry to Kibbutz Ein Gev, and after an enjoyable lunch at its restaurant on the seashore, we cross the width of the Sea of Galilee back to Tiberias by boat. As we approach Tiberias, we enjoy a landscape of sparkling waters surrounded by palms.

This region has many resort spots for the young and old alike. During spring and summer months, the Sea is filled with kayaks, sailboats and wind gliders. Among the eucalyptus trees we encounter countless families picnicking on the shores. The beaches along the Sea of Galilee are today the most popular and active vacation spots in the Galilee, and perhaps in all of Israel. Every year, national sports, the Galilee March, the Swim across the Sea, and the International Sea of Galilee Marathon are held in this area.

above: *Palm trees on the shore of the Sea of Galilee*

above right: *Kibbutz Ein Gev fish restaurant, with Mt. Susita in the background*

below: *Bird's eye view of Kibbutz Ein Gev on the Sea of Galilee*

opposite - above and below:
Picnicking and water sports on the sea of Galilee
overleaf - page 52
above: *Swimming across the Sea of Galilee*
below: *Zemach water park*
overleaf - page 53
The Jordan valley with the Golan in the background

HAMMAT GADER

High in the Hills of the Golan, where the Israeli, Syrian and Jordanian borders meet, we come across Hammat Gader. A large park with a man-made warm-water lake at its center is located here. There is also an "alligator lake" populated by hundreds of alligators especially imported from Florida.

The luxurious Roman Baths, the Roman theatre, and the synagogue dating back to the sixth century have all been restored. New bath houses have also been built.

There are four springs in Hamat Gader whose waters contain radon, radium and hydrogen sulphide - the temperatures range from 29-51^0 centigrade.

Modern facilities have once again turned this beauty spot into a popular site for recreation and relaxation.

above left: *At the Alligator park, Hammat Gader*
below: *The warm water lake*
opposite
above right: *fish ponds at Hammat Gader*
above left: *Minaret of the Syrian mosque*
below: *bird's eye view of the Roman bath houses*

YARDENIT

This spot, where the Jordan leaves the Sea of Galilee, has been a holy Christian site from early times. It has undergone renewal since the late 19th century. David Roberts' famous 1839 painting depicts pilgrims gathered to immerse themselves in the holy waters of the Jordan River. Numerous 19th century artists painted this baptismal scene at Yardenit; when the camera was invented in the mid 19th century, it became a very popular photographic subject as well. Today, a modern, built-up Yardenit welcomes visitors from far and wide.

We have arrived! Members of the kibbutz welcome the pilgrims among us, offering us long white robes so that we might be baptised in the Jordan waters. Thus we join the millions of Christians who have come from all corners of the world to participate in the traditional ceremony.

pages 56, 57: Views of Yardenit

BETH SHEAN

Beth Shean, called after a Canaanite deity, is already mentioned in ancient Egyptian writings. Beth Shean is mentioned in the Bible the first time after the battle of Gilboa in connection with Samuel's death. In past years, Beth Shean has been very intensively excavated. The fertile surroundings of this town have always drawn many people, especially Romans and Greeks. They called the city Skythopolis. In Beth Shean is to be found the best preserved Roman amphitheatre in Israel, with overpowering acoustics. Opposite rises the hill fortress of the city: in the south can be seen the excavations of a Canaanite temple of Astarte, in the north a temple of Dagon.

Beth Shean, bird's eye view of excavations.

JORDAN VALLEY

From this point the Jordan river flows slowly, winding in countless twists and turns southward past the Beth Shean Valley until it reaches the Dead Sea. In the past, there was one large lake extending from the hills in the Galilee until the Dead Sea in the south. Over the course of thousands of years natural phenomena separated the waters, creating the sweet-water Sea of Galilee and the very salty Dead Sea, situated at the lowest point on the globe.

For hundreds of years, residents of the region tried to divert the sweet waters of the Jordan for drinking, irrigation, and for generating electrical energy. These efforts are evident at the place where the Yarmuk River which descends from the heights of Hammat Gader meets the Jordan - a spot called Naharayim. The first settlers who returned to this spot in the late 19th and early 20th centuries succeeded in developing this region and turning it into one of Israel's luscious green gardens.

Along the southern shores of the Sea of Galilee and along the Jordan River which descends into the Dead Sea, pioneers established tens of kibbutzim and settlements, capitalising on the warm climate and the sweet Jordan waters to grow banana and date palms. From here we can also travel to Jerusalem, passing the famous city of Jericho on the way.

UPPER GALILEE

If you have experienced the heavy heat and still wish to remain in the Galilee, return to Tiberias for a rest, and then take off once again for the Upper Galilee. You will discover that the air in the evergreen forests of the Upper Galilee is much clearer and cooler.

Up in the Golan Heights, some 600 metres above the Sea of Galilee, the weather, the flora and the fauna are drastically different. Israel's water sources are few, and therefore very important. The springs in the north - the Dan and the Hatzbani, are our sources of life. Aside from the ancient cities of Tiberias and Safed, three new cities have been added to the landscape of the Upper Galilee: Hazor, Kiryat Shmona and Carmiel. These small cities are surrounded by smaller settlements and kibbutzim, most of whose residents engage in agriculture and high-tech industry.

previous - page 59
above: Two bridges over the River Jordan near kibbutz Gesher
below: The River Jordan near Naharayim

above: *The Huleh valley and the Golan Heights with snow-covered Mt. Hermon in the background*
above right: *River Jordan with Mt. Hermon in the background*
below right: *Ayelet Hashachar Kibbutz Guest House*

METULLAH

We have reached Metullah, the settlement on the Lebanese border. Facing us is Mount Hermon, which is covered with snow most of the year. From this mountain, the highest spot in Israel, one can see almost all of Israel, as well as neighboring Syria, Lebanon, Jordan and even the Mediterranean Sea and the Sea of Galilee.

SAFED

The hometown of Jewish mysticism or 'kabbala' - Safed nestles high in the green mountains of Upper Galilee. Once the home of scholars and sages - it is more well-known today as one of the main centres for art and handicrafts.

The cool, clean mountain air, the wonderful scenery and the proximity of interesting sites to visit make Safed a popular summer resort for both Israelis and overseas holiday makers.

left: The Banias water fall
below: The Dan stream; one of the three sources of the River Jordan
opposite
above: Metulla, general view
below left: The Tanur water fall
below right: The Trumpeldor Memorial at Tel Hai

Israel is a tiny country when viewed on a map of the world. But nature has blessed her with a unique topography of mountains and valleys, plains and deserts. The climate is likewise diverse: snow in the high mountains and on the Hermon; cold, clear air in the north; oppressive heat in the Jordan Valley and desert climate in the Negev and in the Judean Wilderness.

This small strip of land between the Mediterranean Sea and the Syrian desert, between the Sinai Desert and Africa and Asia was a major crossroad in ancient history. This little country at the center of the globe played an important role in the history of the three great religions - Judaism, Christianity and Islam.

Now having traveled through the Galilee, and visited its holy sites, it is not difficult to understand the awesome reverence that infuenced the work of writers and poets, their yearnings satisfied after their pilgrimage to the Holy Land.

left: *A lane in old Safed*
below: *Bird's eye view of Safed, capital of Upper Galilee, with Mt. Meron in the background*